CONTENTS

CHAPTER 1

WHAT IS HYDROPOWER?

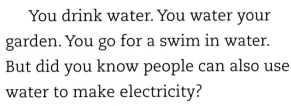

FACT

Electricity from hydropower costs less than many other forms of energy. It can be made for one-third the cost of electricity made using fossil fuels.

You drink water. You water your garden. You go for a swim in water. But did you know people can also use water to make electricity?

Hydro is the Greek word for "water". Hydropower uses water to make electricity. Hydropower is also called hydroelectricity. It is a **renewable** energy source.

Renewable energy is made using resources that cannot be used up. Solar power comes from the Sun. Wind power comes from the wind. Geothermal power comes from heat inside Earth. These are all forms of renewable energy.

Coal, oil and natural gas are non-renewable resources. These fossil fuels take hundreds of millions of years to form. At some point, these fuel sources will be used up.

....

renewable describes power from sources that you can use again and again that cannot be used up, such as wind, water and sun

HYDROPOWER THROUGHOUT HISTORY

Hydropower is not new. People have used water power for more than 2,000 years. The ancient Greeks used flowing water to turn paddle wheels. The wheels helped grind wheat into flour. By the 1700s water was powering grain, timber, iron and fabric mills. The earliest paddle wheels were wooden. During the 1700s people began using larger iron wheels. These larger wheels could make more power. This meant factories could make more goods in less time.

An old mill still stands along the river in Bayeux, France.

The first mills used the power of water to do work. But they could not store that energy as electricity.

Soon scientists learned how to use hydropower to create electricity. The world's first hydroelectric project powered a single lamp in England in 1878. Four years later, the world's first hydroelectric power station began operating. It was located in Appleton, Wisconsin, USA. The plant provided its own power needs and supplied power to two nearby buildings. By 1886 there were between 40 and 50 hydropower stations in North America.

HYDROPOWER TODAY

Today hydropower is the world's most popular type of renewable energy. Hydropower stations range in size. The largest power stations can make enough power for more than 20,000 households. Micro power stations may create just enough power for one home or farm. There are more than 8,200 large hydropower stations around the world.

The Krasnoyarsk Dam in Russia supplies power to the nearby aluminium works.

POWERED BY THE WATER CYCLE

Hydropower relies on Earth's natural water cycle. The water cycle includes:

Evaporation – Energy from the Sun warms water on Earth's surface. Some of the water turns into **vapour**. This is called evaporation. Plants and trees also lose water through their leaves. This process is called transpiration.

Condensation – As water vapour rises, it cools and turns back into liquid. The liquid joins with particles in the air to form clouds.

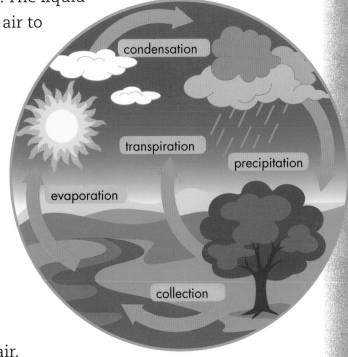

Precipitation – When the drops in the clouds become too heavy for the air to hold them, they fall back to Earth as rain, snow, hail or sleet.

Collection – When precipitation falls, it flows into oceans, rivers, lakes and ponds.

Eventually, this water evaporates back into the air. Then the cycle starts again.

....

vapour gas made from a liquid

CHAPTER 2

HOW CAN WATER MAKE ELECTRICITY?

FACT

Washington makes more hydroelectricity than any other US state. The Grand Coulee Dam (pictured) is the largest source of hydroelectricity in the United States. A quarter of Washington's electricity comes from hydropower each year.

You have probably been taught that water and electricity don't mix. For example, blow drying your hair in the bath is an awful idea. If you drop the hairdryer in the water, it could cause a nasty shock or even kill you. So how can water be used to make electricity?

Hydropower isn't dangerous because water does not actually touch the electricity. At most hydropower stations, water is held behind a dam. This water forms an artificial lake called a reservoir. Hydropower stations contain **turbines** that look like fans or propellers. When water is released from the reservoir, it falls through a large pipe. The water spins the turbine blades. The turbines connect to **generators** that also spin. The generators make electricity as they spin. **Transformers** help balance how much electricity is sent out of the power station. Power lines carry the electricity to nearby cities and rural areas.

turbine machine with blades that can be turned by steam or water

generator machine used to convert mechanical energy into electricity

transformer device that changes the force of an electrical current

How much electricity a hydropower station makes depends on how much water flows through the dam and how far it falls. A large, fast river carries more energy than a small, slow one. Also, water falling from a high point, such as Niagara Falls in the United States, can produce more energy than a smaller waterfall. For this reason, most hydropower stations are located in hills or mountains.

Freezing winter temperatures can affect hydropower stations. Large power stations usually have very deep reservoirs. Even if there is ice on the top, the water towards the bottom keeps flowing. Power stations on smaller waterways do not work well in cold weather. The water at these power stations often freezes solid in winter. Smaller power stations located in cold climates usually work only during warm weather.

The water in Niagara Falls drops nearly 61 metres (200 feet) in some places.

There are three types of hydropower stations. Working out which type is right for an area depends on land features, climate and energy needs.

Impoundment – This type of power station is also called a "reservoir" system. It is the most common type of hydropower station. These power stations use dams to store river water in reservoirs. When water is released, it flows through turbines. They spin a generator to make electricity. Dam gates adjust to allow more or less water to flow through.

Diversion – These are also known as "run of the river" power stations. They have no reservoirs. They generate power using the natural flow of river water to spin turbines.

Pumped storage – Pumped storage power stations work like giant batteries. They can combine solar, wind and hydropower. When the sun is shining and the wind is blowing, extra electricity can be produced from wind and solar power. Pumped storage power stations make use of this extra power. Pumps powered by the extra wind and solar electricity bring water from a lower reservoir to a higher reservoir. When more power is needed, water is released back into the lower reservoir through turbines.

FACT

Pumped storage power stations can also be used with nuclear power.

the Kruonis Pumped Storage Hydroelectric Power Station in Lithuania

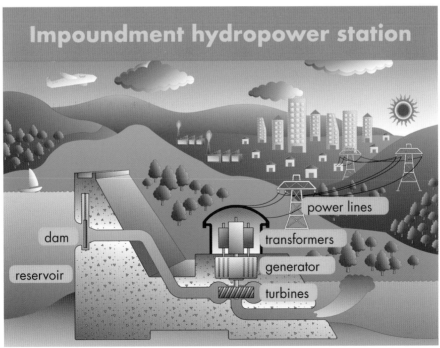

Impoundment hydropower station

dam

reservoir

power lines

transformers

generator

turbines

CHAPTER 3

HYDROPOWER PROS AND CONS

Power stations burning fossil fuels release harmful chemicals into the air.

People have burned fossil fuels to make energy for many years. These fuels provide power for electricity and transport, but they have drawbacks. Burning coal, oil and natural gas pollutes the air and makes people unwell. Coal dust can cause illness in people who work in mines or live nearby. Leaks from oil pipelines or tankers can damage the environment and kill wildlife. Natural gas catches fire easily, which makes it dangerous to **transport**. Plus, fossil fuels will one day run out. Renewable energy sources are available, safe and better for the environment. They are also becoming more affordable.

....

transport move or carry something or someone from one place to another

Killer oil spill

The world's largest oil spill happened in 1991 in the Persian Gulf. One barrel of crude oil holds 159 litres (42 gallons). About 10 million barrels of oil spilled across an area 160 kilometres (100 miles) long and 64 kilometres (40 miles) wide. The oil killed countless fish and about 30,000 water birds.

Hydropower now supplies 71 per cent of the world's renewable electricity. It has been used for many years, so people trust it. It is also one of the cheapest ways to produce power. Like any power source, however, it has both advantages and disadvantages.

POSITIVES OF HYDROPOWER

Hydropower has many benefits. It's fuelled by water, so it doesn't pollute the air the way that power stations burning fossil fuels do. Hydropower is also flexible. Water flow can be adjusted to create a little power or a lot of it. An area with a hydropower station can produce its own energy. That means residents do not have to rely on fuel being transported from other areas or countries. This cuts down on pollution as well.

The Riga Electric Hydropower Station in Latvia has been in operation since the 1970s.

NEGATIVES OF HYDROPOWER

Hydropower isn't a perfect energy source. It takes lots of water and land to build a hydropower station. To build reservoirs, land must be flooded. If people live on that land, they must move from their homes. Once a good location has been found, the cost of building the power station can be extremely expensive. It can reach billions of pounds.

Hydropower is also dependent on the weather cycle. Power can't be produced when there's a long dry spell.

Building a hydroelectric power station can greatly change the natural environment.

Fish such as salmon swim upstream to lay their eggs.

Many people also have concerns about the ways hydropower stations affect the environment. Dams can raise river temperatures. The warmer water may kill off certain types of plants and fish. Dams also interfere with some fish **migration**. When these fish can't swim up or down stream, they can't **reproduce**.

migration regular movement of animals from one place to another

reproduce breed and have offspring

HELPING FISH AROUND DAMS

If fish can't swim to where they need to go, they may become ill or not be able to reproduce. Entire species can die off. But scientists are working to solve this problem.

Fish ladders provide **detours** around dams. The ladders contain a series of small pools laid out like stairs. Fish leap through gushing water and land in a pool. They rest there for a while before leaping into the next pool. They repeat the process until they are past the dam.

Fish lifts can also help fish get around dams. Fish swim into a container at the base of a dam. When enough fish gather, the container carries them over the dam. The fish are then released.

Fish ladders are part of the Bonneville Dam in Oregon, USA.

detour route to travel on when the usual way of travelling cannot be used

The fish ladder at this hydroelectric power station in Germany creates a path that makes it easier for the fish to follow.

Many uses for dams

In the United States, only 2,400 of the country's 80,000 dams make electricity. So what are all those other dams used for? Many dams hold local water supplies. This water may be cleaned and used for drinking and bathing. They can provide water for swimming, boating or for farmers to water their crops. Some dams raise water levels enough so that ships can travel where it would otherwise be too shallow. Other dams work to prevent floods. During heavy rains, dam gates can be closed to store water in the reservoir. During dry weather, gates can be opened to release water and raise river levels.

CHAPTER 4

HOW AND WHERE IS HYDROPOWER USED?

Hydropower is the most widely used renewable energy source. About 71 per cent of the world's renewable energy comes from hydropower. More than 150 countries create it. China makes more hydroelectricity than any other country. Hydropower makes one-fifth of all electricity in the world.

Top hydropower-generating countries

Country	billion kWh
China	1,103*
Canada	377*
Brazil	356*
United States	249*
Russia	166*
Norway	137*
India	120*
Japan	85*
Sweden	75*
Venezuela	74*

*billion kWh

Large amounts of energy are measured by kilowatt hour (kWh). A kWh is equal to 1,000 watts of power for one hour. A billion kWh is an even larger measurement. It is equal to one billion times 1,000 watts per hour. One 100-watt light bulb would take 10 hours to use 1 kWh of energy. It would take 1 billion of those light bulbs burning for 10 hours to use 1 billion kWh.

FACT

The Three Gorges Dam on China's Yangtze River is the world's largest hydropower dam. The dam is more than 1.6 kilometres (1 mile) wide.

LOOKING TO THE FUTURE

Many people want to reduce pollution and protect natural resources. They turn to renewable energy sources to help in these efforts. Hydropower may soon play an even larger role in making energy throughout the world.

Hydroelectric dams sit on some of the world's most powerful rivers. Yet there are many places where new dams could be built. Central America, South America, central Africa, India and China may be good areas for growth.

Many more hydroelectric dams such as this one in Ecuador are being planned along the Amazon River in South America.

Scientists and engineers are experimenting with better ways to build dams and make more power with existing dams. New turbines are being designed to safely make more power. Researchers are trying to add turbines to dams that weren't built for power. Others are working on ways to use ocean waves to make electricity. As technology improves, hydropower will be even more available and affordable.

In Norway, wave converters are already providing electricity for the residents of its towns and cities.

COULD YOU WORK AT A HYDROPOWER STATION?

In 2016 more than 8 million people worldwide worked in the field of renewable energy. This number is expected to keep growing. Could you become one of those people?

Many engineers and electricians are needed to work at hydropower stations. Workers are needed to keep the power station running smoothly and repair equipment. Many of these jobs require university degrees in fields such as engineering or physics. How you feel about your maths and science lessons now can help you decide if you like these subjects.

Hydropower stations also employ support staff. These employees don't run the turbines, but their work is important. For example, wildlife biologists make sure the power stations do not harm fish or animals. Recreation employees design programmes for boaters and swimmers to enjoy the water without interfering with the operation of the dam. There are also spokespeople to share messages about the power station. If you want to work at a hydropower station one day, there are many possibilities!

FACT

The hydroelectricity industry is growing fast. Projections show it could double by the year 2050.

GLOSSARY

detour route to travel on when the usual way of travelling cannot be used

generator machine used to convert mechanical energy into electricity

migration regular movement of animals from one place to another

renewable describes power from sources that you can use again and again that cannot be used up, such as wind, water and sun

reproduce breed and have offspring

transformer device that changes the force of an electrical current

transport move or carry something or someone from one place to another

turbine machine with blades that can be turned by steam or water

vapour gas made from a liquid

FIND OUT MORE

BOOKS

From Falling Water to Electric Car: An energy journey through the world of electricity (Energy Journeys), Ian Graham (Raintree, 2015)

How Renewable Energy Works (Eco Works), Geoff Barker (Franklin Watts, 2017)

Sustainable Energy (Let's Think About...), Vic Parker (Raintree, 2015)

WEBSITES

www.bbc.com/bitesize/articles/ztxwqty
Learn more about renewable and non-renewable energy.

www.dkfindout.com/uk/science/electricity/generating-electricity
Find out more about how electricity is generated and different sources of energy.

DISCUSSION QUESTIONS

1. More than 75 per cent of the world's energy still comes from fossil fuels. Why don't more countries rely upon renewable energy sources such as hydropower?

2. What do you think will happen if people keep using fossil fuels instead of renewable energy sources?

3. There are pros and cons to using hydropower. Do you think the advantages outweigh the disadvantages?

INDEX

Fact Finders®

ENERGY REVOLUTION

HYDROPOWER

By Mary Boone

Raintree is an imprint of Capstone Global Library Limited, a company incorporated in
England and Wales having its registered office at 264 Banbury Road, Oxford, OX2 7DY –
Registered company number: 6695582

www.raintree.co.uk
myorders@raintree.co.uk

Text © Capstone Global Library Limited 2020
The moral rights of the proprietor have been asserted.

Edited by Mandy Robbins
Designed by Terri Poburka
Original illustrations © Capstone Global Library Limited 2020
Picture research by Jo Miller
Production by Kathy McColley
Originated by Capstone Global Library Ltd
Printed and bound in India

ISBN 978 1 4747 6990 7 (hardcover)
ISBN 978 1 4747 6996 9 (paperback)

British Library Cataloguing in Publication Data
A full catalogue record for this book is available from the Britis

Acknowledgements
We would like to thank the following for permission to reproduce photographs:
Alamy: imageBROKER, 23, Robert Matton AB, 27, Xinhua, 24-25; Getty Images: Langevin
Jacques/Contributor, 17, (inset); iStockphoto: MarioGuti, 20; Newscom: Xinhua Agency/
Pan Siwei, 29; Shutterstock: 3xy, 9, A. Aleksandravicius, 15 (top), Aleks Kend, 19, Ariel
Ukulele, 26, bubblea, 15; (bottom), Canadapanda, 21, Edmund Lowe Photography, 10-11,
Evgeny Vorobyev, 8, Hampi, 25, lexaarts, 16-17, Looka, 7, maxi_kore, 13, Nick_Nick, 6,
Rigucci, 22, snapgalleria, 11, stocksolutions, Cover, Tom Wang, 4-5: Design Elements:
Shutterstock: HAKKI ARSLAN, T.Sumaetho.